The Ultimate Handbook for tne Dom and
Sub: Training for the Serious Pain and
Discipline Seekers

Table of Contents

Introduction

Do you have a sub that you've managed to train pretty well, but you want to take this to the next level? That's often something that a lot of times, people want to learn more about. There are much harder levels of BDSM to explore, and this book will give you what you want to know about this.

By the end of this, you'll learn how to train your sub for ultimate pleasure, and for higher levels of pain. Now, it's best to make sure that you've already discussed a majority of this with your sub, and you can really benefit from this in a mutual manner. It's definitely a fun adventure, but it's actually something that you need to discuss with your partner before you do.

However, if you're ready to take on this adventure, and you want to really explore this, you totally can. This book will give you more advanced, and expert tips on how to train your sub for pleasure. We will go over many different parts of this, and also the psychology behind how to train your sub to listen to your every command.

BDSM is an adventure, and you're about to go on it with a trustworthy partner. So, you'll be able to really understand what needs to be a part of this, and how to really ensure that you get the best from this.

You may wonder what you need to do in order to make your sex slave the best that it can be. If you're looking to train this sub, you should know a few things that you will want to have in play. This is especially important if you're going to be controlling every aspect of their lives.

The Few Things to learn

When choosing to be a submissive, the best thing to do is to realize what you're getting into. Being a slave might not seem like it's something that you want, but lots of times, it actually involves different aspects that you may be interested in. Lots of times, people may want this for a little while, or some want it 24/7.

At the beginning, you may want to only be a slave for initial scenes, such as roleplaying and such. You may not want this all the time, and if that's the case, that's totally okay, and you can actively choose with your dom what you want.

You may need to also learn how to be honest with what you want. It has to be yes and no with people, not just maybes, and you should choose what you want, and when you do, you should be honest. You shouldn't agree to something that you're not sure of. With slave training, there should always be a chance that you may not want it all the time, so you should always ask yourself the hard questions before you go in, and to understand realities.

If you've been thinking of going into 24/7 slave training, you should always remember that you're putting your life in the control of another being, and while roleplaying might be good for the moment, if you're going to be permanent, the master will have full control. But, if the scene is over, you should definitely go back to normal.

Now, if you're going to do this 24/7, just know that every single aspect of your life is something your master will control. For example, if you start to like music, the master might change it to something that you don't enjoy, and you may have to give up other things. Lots of times, the master will permit you to do other things at times, but if you're interested in having these limitations that you may have, then this might be for you.

For many subs, this also goes into certain colors, scents, or even what your master may dress you in. Some people may like it if their master did this, but this takes some getting used to. Sometimes, the master may put you in some skimpy outfits, or maybe something modest. Lots of times this is a new feeling, but lots of times, people who are interested in the being controlled aspect do enjoy this,

This isn't just in what you want to wear or not wear, it can involve different tasks, and that may be a lot more. Lots of times, you may take care of possessions, and you're given tasks that are fitting to your capabilities.

Lots of times though, the sex slave lifestyle does actually stand at the forefront. If you're not sure of whether you want this, you shouldn't go into it. Lots of people walk into this think it's just serving the guy, but sometimes it's more than that.

Choosing to engage in BDSM slavery can be a bit of a shocking thing, and ideally, if you're not ready to fully immerse into that lifestyle. It's a different way to live, since lots of times, you have to learn self-discipline, how to say things in the relationship, and how to not let your temper go off the deep end.

For some, they might think that this is too hard. But, sometimes it allows you to have a better relationship with your partner. It's an interesting dynamic.

Negotiate First

Obviously, before you get trained into this, you need negotiations, which are the why, what where, when, how, and who, and in essence, this is what you should have in place. It's a set of rules, and the top only uses what they're allowed to have. The top in essence gets a chance to own a portion of the bottom, and at the beginning, they may not have any ownership. Lots of times, these are more about the here and now, and not about the future, but for actual long-term agreements, you need to sit down to figure this out.

The negotiations are used for fulfilling fantasies. Lots of times, meetings may not be interesting, but you need them, since it will actually put into place what's good, and what's not so good. You need to have these in place before you essentially condition your sub into a scene.

They are also used in slave training, which in essence gives the freedoms and restrictions that will be presented, and for how long. You essentially won't fully exchange the power, and there are limits to the where and how, and even when this happens. You can even include how they live, when they visit, services, relationships with others, how long, and what the submissive doesn't give to the master, limits of punishments, any arrangements of money, and even safe words as well. In essence, it's a contractual agreement to help negotiate how their relationship will be.

Lots of times, with the long-term ones, there are boundaries there, and they're contractually agreed upon. The submissive does have some control, and the dominant has limits to this as well.

The Choice Decision

When you're using the master-sex slave relationship, the slave allows the master to make the choices. The sub is in essence allowing themselves to be the property, and he will give the sub anything that they want. It's not negotiations, but instead the slave accepting the slavery, losing the freedoms, and being owned by the master. Now, there isn't abuse, or anything that is illegal done with these obviously. In essence, this is surrendering the freedoms in a negotiated agreement. It in essence allows for the slave to give something to the other, to let them do as they wish. These are often very long, and detailed, and they often become less structured, along with shorter too. Lots of times, this simple document expresses ownership in a very brief manner. There is a practical side as well, since the slave does choose what they're giving up, and what they don't give up. While there may be freedoms surrendered, usually the person is with someone that they can trust, and who match their own personal desires.

The form should be used before any scene, and if you're going into this for the long term, you should have this.

The Ideal Master

Usually, there are a few aspects that a master should have. It's important that they understand this, because a good master will take care and understand the dynamics of the relationship. Bad ones bring forth arguments, and potentially other messes.

So what are some of the aspects? Well, read on.

The first thing that the master should understand, is the psychology of the person, the property in a sense. The person should know how to understand what a person thinks, and not just the slavery and submission aspects, but about anything they'd like to share. The master will want full control over this, and you have to understand the person fully so that you can understand the motives of the slave in a clear manner.

The master should also learn about new subjects, and be trained on these subjects. It will also prevent boredom.

Having humor should also be a good thing, including seeing the absurdity of the situations and also knowing that this is silly, and that they should be able to see that this isn't an actual slave and owner relationship, but actually something that they are in together. You also need to be flexible, and keep the relationship nice and fresh, since the dynamics do change over time. You don't want the slave to feel like they're being smothered, so do make sure to change it up over time.

You should also make sure that there are future plans there, and if you don't have those in place before you begin, it can create a problem. Life does involve some trials, including getting sick, death, and even divorce if you're married. If you do have these happen, make sure that there is equitable assets sharing, and make sure that the slave can still take care of this when the master passes. With health care, you should always have it at the forefront, and make sure that both partners can take care of themselves. Do have contingency plans in for the long term and discuss this with the slave.

You should also be capable of love, and this may change the dynamic, since it might stop the sharing and other actions. The master should be cognizant of this.

And finally, the master should also know about the desires of the slave, and make sure to act accordingly. You don't have to give into these all the time, but they're something that should be acknowledged in some way, shape or form.

Slavespace

You may have heard of subspace, which is something that often happens in BDSM scenes, where it essentially creates a conscious, uninhibited plane. It's a very mind-expanding experience. Lots of submissives go for this, being engulfed in these free time ideas, and lots of times, the fantasies of being under control can be taken a step further with slave training. Subspace allows for the person to let go, with wanton sexuality at the forefront, and it creates a very great state of relaxation in the person.

You can learn to control the subspace too, and lots of times, you can put your own mind into it, and it is quite an interesting stimulation. When you get accepted as a slave, and living like one, you can experience a new type of subspace. It can be a very strange feeling, especially if you're in isolation. Sometimes when you get a punishment during slave training, it can make you feel this.

Now it does cause you to feel many different emotions, a gamut of them ranging from sadness and feeling sorry for yourself, hope that you'd be let out early, and then suddenly you start to feel the discomfort go away. It then causes a responsibility for the actions themselves to come about.

Then there is slave space, which in essence is emotional detachment, and acceptance of the situation. You start to not feel sorry for yourself, and you don't feel emotional. It allows you to form a proper apology, and understand the slave training. It's a different type of space, and in this, you start to think of the master, and your mind doesn't wander, and you don't take everything personally. Slavespace does become easier each time. Slavespace is different though because subspace is mostly based on reactions and feelings, focusing on yourself. With slavespace, it's focusing on others, and mostly on contentment and pleasure from serving. It's not as selfish in a sense. It's something that a sub may feel while they're in slave training.

Adapting to slave Training

Slave training is definitely hard at first, and in a sexual sense, it can definitely be a bit of a jarring situation. There are a few things that you should definitely keep in mind in order to make sure that you have a proper experience, and to have the best training possible.

- Learn to listen: do ask questions and learn about some of the different aspects of it. Do observe both verbal and non-verbal communication.

- Observe: being able to observe what does please and not please the master is a key part of this, since detail is often a huge part of this.

- Know what's going on: This is something that you do need to get better with in many cases. Lots of times, people don't understand what's going on, and this can cause major mistakes. Communication is key, and if you have a question, do ask about it.

- Don't overly evaluate or judge: this is new, and compared to vanilla relationships, it'd different. You do need to learn how to obey without judging, since the master is a big part of the correcting of actions and such.

- Curiosity is key: curiosity is how you understand what you're going through, and you'll be more open to learn. Do be open because if you reveal your thoughts and emotions to the master that you trust, it can make it better.

- Become involved: learn the rules and study them, and practice what the master wants out of you. don't expect the master to hold your hand.

- Expect to get frustrated: This isn't easy or natural, but if you recognize this, you'll be able to deal with them easily. Opening up about this is good, and you should learn new habits and get rid of the old ones.

- Learn to accept criticism: you may have to change behaviors and attitudes, and you may get challenged by the master, so expect him to be critical.

- Expect to change: you will change your behavior, thoughts, and emotions, among other things. Prepare for the change, and expect to be molded into the way the master desires. It can help you a lot.

- Be obedient: do listen to the master, and since obedience is learned, you'll be able to improve your skills. Be consistent with this.

- Be devoted: you'll be able to grow with this.

Being open to adapting to slave training is a huge part of this, and for both the slave and the master, it's a huge role to play.

Managing the Slave

Now in the sense of the master, you do need to make sure that you manage the slave well. You'll get to teach her new skills and techniques. If you're going to have her as a sex slave, train her, if you're going to add domestic to her repertoire, add that as well. She can be trained however you want.

As a new dominant, the master must make sure that the slave does have some training in all of this too. If you're worried about something potentially not being safe, do make sure that you understand that you should get help as necessary for this.

In a sense, the master is the personal trainer for the slave. You know like a physical personal trainer? Well take that, and apply it to the slave's goals and future. The training methods are good for this, and the core form of this is based on logic and reason. It's definitely good to understand that you're the one who will be training the slave into the shape that you want to be in.

As a dominant, you need to have a dominant personality, a character that the sub can trust, and have good foundation skills. Be realistic with the wants and needs, and it's important to understand that you do know these, and work on whether or not you want to cater to these desires.

As a master, you've got different modes for the slave, and they are as follows:

- Slave mode

- At Ease mode

- Service mode

with slave mode, in essence the slave will be managed by you. In this, they're not allowed to speak without you telling them, and the slave needs to have permission for everything, and it puts together the slave/master structure. The slave should know that they are or aren't allowed to have different items, oftentimes without clothing. The slave listens to the master, uses "yes sir" and asks for permission with everything.

In service mode, the slave does still present to the master, but isn't restrictive, and this allows for the slave to develop further into the slave mode, not just the service mode. This can help the slave also get acclimated to elements such as presenting, saying different things like "yes sir" and also understanding the lifestyle.

At-ease is just that, where you're not having the slave do this. The scene is off, and the person doesn't have to be in either mode.

For the master, you should help the slave get into this, and show them the path that they need to take. It's important to really understand this so you can communicate it to the slave in an effective manner.

This chapter discussed slave training in both a sexual, and a non-sexual way, so do make sure that you take all of this into consideration, and understand just what it takes to be in this lifestyle.

Chapter 2: Piercing play and How to Go About Engaging in It

Another interesting type of play that you may be curious about is piercing play. Piercings are often something that people enjoy getting for bodily decoration in a permanent sense, but piercing play is a way to induce pleasure in a BDSM scene in a different way. While it does involve piercings, the needles, bones, and other tools that are used when you are piercing often are removed once the scene is over, so the wounds will heal.

Why Engage in It

Lots of times, play piercing is a bit misunderstood, mostly because hey, you're changing the way your body looks for pleasure. But, piercings also are done to help express yourself, tribal rituals, discovery, sexual pleasure, or even entertainment.

In the realm of BDSM, play piercing allows for endorphin highs, which can induce incredible orgasms in people that try this. The idea of multiple piercings in a way that's erotically or spiritually charged is quite different in a sense. It's different than going to the doctor and getting a shot, because the needle is through the skin so that both ends are accessible rather than just the skin itself.

Piercing Play Vs. What Needle Play Is

You may wonder if these are the same thing. The answer, they're not. Piercing play involves the stimulation of the piercings with the hands, mouth, toys, or stimulation devices, but needle play involves piercings to the partner's areas to stimulate them. Obviously, you should make sure that with both of these, you do practice good safety and hygiene, and also have the right supplies.

Needle Play safety and Needle information

When you're getting into needle play, you should always make sure both of you are tested. Before you begin, talk about any diseases that are transmitted via blood, and make sure you're tested for these. Always make sure that you have disinfectants, a container for the needles, play pricing needles, and gloves to protect your hands, and gauze and other first aid items to help when there is too much blood. Make sure that you're not allergic to the items that you're going to use, including alcohol and iodine.

When using these, you should first and foremost always attend a workshop or a class on needle play, and also talking to your partner to know about what sorts of insertion techniques are for you. You should use either fine-gauge hypodermic needles to help with leverage, acupuncture needles since these rarely draw blood, piercing needles, and dental needles that you can use with both needle play and electronic stimulation. Use the first option for needle play in general, but you can determine what works for you based on your own personal comfort.

Always make sure that you do have everything packaged and sterilized, and you should use sterile needles each time you do this.

How to engage in Needle play

When you're starting needle play, always talk about the risks. If you're doing this, put the partner laying down so that it doesn't case too much blood to come out. Have them wear a dental bib. After that, put on gloves, and clean the piercing area. If you're going to make a design, use little skin markers.

Once ready, start to put the needle near the area that you're piercing. You should use the 20-22g needles to pierce tougher skin, and then use the finer gauges to use it on tender areas. Pinch the area, insert the needle with the beveled area up, horizontal, and make sure not to angle it so that it doesn't go too deep. You can use a cork or a thimble to prevent your hands from being poked. Once the needles are put in, you can then stimulate the partner, simply by flossing the needles, flicking them, slapping them with a plastic wrap over the needles, or even a vibrator. You can use heat and coolness, or even electronic stimulation. Sensation play is often a key part here.

Once this is done, you should soak some gauze pads, and then put them on the needles. Remove and push down gently on the gauze. It'll help the blood clot, reduce bruising and swelling, and clean the area. Make sure pull them out swiftly, but horizontally, and from there, dispose of them.

Piercing play Process

When you're getting into piecing play, it doesn't require much prep work. Make sure that your hands are clean, along with your partner's, and then gently pull on them, twist, apply weights, or even electrostimulation on the areas. It's quite nice if you have genital or nipple piercings to work with.

Now with permanent piercings, you should avoid anywhere near the eyes, and make sure that you talk to your partner while you're doing this so that you're not hurting them. Make sure to check in with them when you do this.

Now with needle play that involves play piercing, you want something that's very fine gauge, with the higher numbers being finer. You should make sure that they can be put onto the skin in an easy manner, and usually, the syringe needles are easier to insert, because you can use pressure on this without forcing it too much. However, those that are fine are much harder to manipulate, so they could get in deep. If you're going for tougher areas, always make sure they're heavier. You should remove them each at a time from the package and then insert. Always check to make sure there aren't any defects, and get rid of the imperfect ones. Sometimes, pinching the skin is good. You should make sure that if you go deep, you have a cloth to get the excess blood.

The best piercing areas

So what are the best piercing areas? Well, lots of times, people like the butt, back, breasts, abdomen, genitals, and thighs, and you can insert them essentially anywhere other than the eyes. If you want to create an interesting pattern with this, always work from the top down, through the area that's pierced so that you don't poke yourself. If you notice that the blood wells up, do give it some gauze and get rid of the bloody gauze. You should try to put them anywhere you feel it looks nice, and you can use a crisscross pattern where you put a needle below where it's placed. There aren't many limits to what you can't do with this.

When it comes to stimulating them with accessories, you can use some floss to lightly pull on these, or even wire or lace through corset piercings. If you've ever seen those, usually they're done with a crisscross pattern. Adult toys such as weights, vibrators, and floggers do definitely help enhance the sensation.

Reminder that, with this, if you do end up twisting or pulling them, it causes sensation, so be careful.

Now, if you really want to get into an extreme form of BDSM, there is something called flash hook suspension, where the person is suspended vertically or horizontally with hooks through the flesh, and it's done as a rite of passage, and it's used in rituals more than anything.

As always, if you're going for the more extreme levels, you should always carry this out with the appropriate type of person for this.

The Aftercare

Once you're done, you should have the person who was being pierced use soap and warm water. If you expose the area to air, it'll speed up the healing process, but also do make sure you've got ointments, adhesives, and the like. The marks tend to last about a week, and you may notice some bruising. If you see signs of an infection, do contact a professional immediately.

Sometimes if you accidentally get pricked with the needle, it may cause you to freak out. First, take off the gloves, and wish it with soap and water, and get tested. If you struck yourself before the needle was removed, then you won't have to remove it, but usually it's still in the person's skin. If you do notice this, you can reduce the risk of bodily fluid exposure by sliding it through the skin. You can put a cork into the point and then get the hub of it out with cutters and remove it from the cork side. You should use EMIT sheers if you can't remove it.

Finally, if you notice a lot of blood when you're done piercing, you should consult a professional, since you may have clipped a vessel. If that's the case, you may have pierced near the nipples, since it's got a lot of blood vessels there.

If you like blood play, you can sometimes enjoy I, and from there, you should cover it with gauze and continue until its stopped. You may bruise up, but that's not a bad thing.

Piercing play is something that you may be into, and needle play might be something you find erotically stimulating. If you've ever been curious, do consider maybe trying it, but only with a person who knows what they're doing, and how to effectively take care of it.

One aspect of BDSM that some people get interested in, is fisting. While it may be impossible for some, some people love it. It's a very intimate action, and it's a very interesting, and impactful penetrative sexual act. You obviously need to be careful with this, since it is a very intimate action, and often, it's a very interesting activity. You can do it both vaginally and anally, and we will discuss how you do both.

The Risks

The first thing we will highlight are the risks. Let's get it all out in the open. There is the chance of possible tearing, abrasions, bruising, and potentially tearing of the vagina. There is also air embolus, and while it's rare, but often possible. A UTI is a very common risk, along with infections that could lead to pelvic inflammatory disease, and some STIs, but those are usually some of the common concerns.

Usually though, this is like worst-case scenario. The vagina is super strong, and you can imagine how much goes into it. With anal, it can often mean anal prolapse, fissure, and tearing, but for the vagina, there are some risks of tearing, but it's often requiring a lot more work to actually cause the tear. Usually, micro tears do cause infection if there is bacteria, but gloves and lubed, along with fingernails that are trimmed help to eliminate this risk.

Another common misconception of this, is that you're going to cause the vagina to get too loose. That's not the case. They're actually versatile and elastic, and we can hold various items inside easily, and you can push babies out and it goes to the same size. It does hurt, but it's actually something that you get used to.

When it comes to the fist, you're not actually putting it in like a fist. It's actually more of a fingers out soft of ordeal. You're not actually going to punch the vagina.

Begin with the buildup.

Now, you do need to make sure that the person who is experiencing the fisting, is actually nice and relaxed. You can't just rush in and put your fist in there. You need to make sure the person is hot and bothered with either hands, a toy, or going down on the person. It's definitely a good thing, because you need to make sure that they're aroused. The vagina naturally lubricates, and that, combined with your own personal lube, will help with improving the experience.

Speaking of Lube.

You need it. This isn't an option here. You also don't want the cheap stuff. What you want here shouldn't be water-based either. Yes it smells like sunshine and flowers, but that stuff dries up fast, and you won't want to hurt the person. Silicone lube is a great one, since it isn't something that sets sticky, and is perfect for condoms too, since if you fuck her after you fist her, it's a good option. The vagina will be sensitive and puffy, so it feels nice.

When it comes to gloves, you want non-latex nitrite gloves, or a medical glove without powder. It's also good to lube these bad boys up too.

Also, clean your fingernails. Or if you have long nails, put cotton balls on there. The last thing they want is for you to be poking and prodding with your long claws in there.

When you're doing this, you should make sure you take this slow, and don't do it quickly, and always communicate with the partner when you receive it.

Is it the whole fist?

The answer, is not necessarily. Lots of times, the hand is quite big, and sometimes anatomy can't accommodate her. Lots of times though,m if the person is super relaxed, you can get the hand in there, but if you can't, then don't despair, especially if it's their first time.

Numbing Agents?

No, just no. Don't bring them to this. Numbing agents are actually not a good idea. Lots of anal fisting ones have that, and with vaginal play, it stops the person from knowing whether or not what they're doing is painful or not. The person being fisted should feel everything, and you should always make sure that if they are uncomfortable, stop it. Numbing gels prevent ideal communication, so you should use them effectively.

With the person, they should be totally aroused, with the tissues of the clit being engorged, and the engorgement is what makes penetration pleasurable. You should definitely utilize check-ins to.

The Steps to Fisting

Now that you've got the person hot and bothered, it's time to get started! First. You want to have the space ready, with some towels to prevent lube spillage, gloves, lube, and toys, and some water and some music and intimate settings.

Now, you want to make sure that all jewelry is removed, and fingers cleaned. The person should empty their bladder, and if there is anal fisting, make sure that you empty down there too or use an enema. An empty bladder also eases the mind, and g-spot stimulation can cause the need to pee as well.

From here, just start to get the person aroused. You want to make sure that they're very warmed up. If they can have an orgasm multiple times, make sure that they do it. Vulva massage, touching the clit, and even stimulating the g-spot are perfect examples.

Now, here comes the penetration. You want to make sure that they're ready, so you always ask first. Seriously, if you don't ask, that does cause the consent to go out, and it can ruin the experience. You start with a finger or two. You want to use clitoral stimulation along with this if they like it. However, some find it distracting, and the one who is fisting can do it if they want. The person who is being fisted might be into touching or using some toys, and having the vibrator near the clit does help with fisting too.

Now, you essentially add fingers. You want to add four of them, getting up to about the knuckle or so, and then hang there for a while. Usually, make sure the partner is loose enough to do this. From here, you tuck the thumb inside, elongate the fist to help minimize the knuckles, and then use light pressure. You want to make sure your hand is totally collapsed, so that the ring finger and the pinky finger collapse in an inward way. This is where you'll want to add a lot of lube. Twisting through each side is a good part of it, and you'll want to work the fist in. It's intense, and you don't want to rush in with this. As always, make sure that communication is at the top of your list of things to do. It the person needs you to stop, you do it.

This is usually the point that either the person gets to, or they don't. If you do make it past there, you do the actual fist. You want to do what feels best, with a slightly upwards motion, going for the g-spot area. You should make sure not to dive completely into the cervix, because that hurts. You should take it very slow, and enjoy the feeling, and always make sure that you check to see if they're good. The motions are supposed to be subtle, not like you're actually punching the vagina, since it's very intense in it of itself.

Now, you want to remove your hand. As always, make sure that you remove this as slowly as you started, and you'll want to collapse the fist and hand to as narrow as possible. You should have the person that's inside guise the hand with their own, and you should very slowly, pull this out of a person. You might need to use your fingers to break suction, and hold it into place as you pull it out. The vagina might try to suck you back in, so be mindful of that.

With this, you'll want to make sure that you do rock it back and forth when you're inserting your hands. This might seem strange, but it actually puts pressure on the internal side of the clitoris, and you can even play at the vaginal opening, with the knuckles in and out, and it's a great sensation.

When it comes to trying out fisting, you can try little rocking and small movements, rocking the knuckles, or whatever you can come up with. As always, make sure that you're really lubed up.

Now, when you're being fisted, it feels extremely sensitive and sore. When you're having sex, you should use a lot of lube, be slow, and drink a ton of water. Sometimes, you may see blood, but it sometimes can stop after a bit. The injuries associated with this are extremely rare, but if you're bleeding for a long time, go to the ER.

When it comes to leaving, you should never try to yank the hand out. It's startling, and extremely painful. Instead, just remain still, massage outside, and slowly relax the muscles. You should also try to use a vibrator while you remove it, since it can help with the overall shock and soreness of anally fisting.

There are times when the person is so shocked that they can't take it all. It happens, and sometimes after doing this, the person may be a bit swollen. That's normal, and it can feel magical, so don't be afraid if that happens.

Afterwards, you always finish off with aftercare. This is super intense, and you should make sure that after such a stimulating activity, you connect with the person. Have them go to the bathroom again and pee, so that they don't get a UTI, have them drink water, eat some of their favorite food, and snuggle or take care of them. You should ask them how they liked it, what they should change, and the like, and it can be a good way to connect with your partner. Try to make sure that you're taken care of.

This is how you fist, and if you do it correctly, you can make the person see stars in the best way possible.

One element that many try to incorporate into the bedroom, is female dominance. It's something that some guys like. The element of relinquishing control in the bedroom is something different for both. Usually, women are the ones to submit to their partner, and the man is the one who dominates. But, what if the roles were reversed? What if you decided to try something a little bit different? Well, read on to find out. It's a form of BDSM that can be a bit different, and you can even take this to extreme levels with stepping, CBT, and other forms, including bondage.

The male/female Dynamic

Lots of times, we kind of stick to the dynamic that the woman is a dainty, pretty princess, and the guy is the one who takes the reins in everything. Our society focuses on the man being the dominant factor, and the woman being the more submissive one. But, did you know that you don't always have to deal with that? That you don't always have to play that role?

it's a bit different for everyone. Some people like it when it's gentle, and may not be into the idea of humiliating their men. It's an interesting power exchange, and it can be a bit different for everyone. When it comes to femdom, usually e think about latex women dominating men, but what you want to be is a woman that enjoys dominating their man, not just for him, but for yourself. It gives you power, and it makes you feel good.

So what are a few things that you should remember? Well, read on to find out a few rules.

The Rules

For the guy, don't push this. Femdom is definitely something that the woman needs to be comfortable with, don't pressure her into doing this, but when she says she's ready, acknowledge it.

You should definitely communicate, and if the scene is done, don't try to ask for more on the man side. Even if it's a compliment, it can make the woman feel like she didn't do it right, so you'll definitely want to be careful.

Don't top from the bottom guys, don't tell her what to do. You want to let the woman take control. In essence, you should tell her that she's got the reins, and you should let her try new things. While the rush is great, you should make sure to give the woman proper encouragement and affection, and if she wants to try it again, do it.

Also, retain dignity in a sense. Submit, but you shouldn't try to be uncomfortable when you submit. Instead, let her see that you're fine with submitting to her. Submission isn't necessarily a bad thing. In a sense, if the man wants to be the sub, and the female is the dominant, he can essentially control what he likes and dislikes, and the woman is able to cater to the man's needs, or deprive him of them for her own personal pleasure.

Now, for the woman, you should make sure that the woman initiates the play, and she starts and stops it when she's good. If she does stop, that's fine. You should communicate after the scene, and talk about how you liked, or disliked something. Feelings tend to come out at a time, and for the woman, it's definitely a new experience.

Now, it does feel good for the woman to try this. It can sometimes be additive to try. Lots of times, women get a taste of being in power, and they in essence want more. You should, if you notice this on the female end, start to feel this way, perhaps back off, and maybe try to lessen the force of the impact from this play. Yes, it does feel good, but also know that sometimes, you can be drunk off the power that's associated with this.

Finally, do have safe words. Just because on the guy end you don't feel like your woman could do something that makes you uncomfortable, doesn't mean that you shouldn't have safe words. Lots of times, guys take this for granted, the woman does something he doesn't enjoy, he ends up getting hurt, and the woman feels bad. Communication and safe words are integral, so please have them in place.

The Basics

There are a few basics that you should keep in mind. These will help with the scenes.

You should first consider blindfolding. That's because, it's easier to feel comfortable and confident doing things when you don't have your partner's eyes on you. Plus, it's a form of domination, and good for sensory play.

Lots of times, you should make sure that you keep the scenario with the female being dominant, and the other one being submissive. It does work in lesbian relationships too, but femdom in that case means that the more "feminine" woman is on top and the more "masculine" is on the bottom. You can always change this though.

Finally, always make sure that you do talk about what you're going to do before you begin. Even something as small as blindfolding and tickling the skin can often shock the person. Bondage is another aspect. You should always, if you do this, make sure that you've discussed the scenario, and discussed the safe word before you continue.

Now, some people like to revolve it around the submissive receiving pleasure, but if you want to have the dominant receive pleasure, that's something too. It really all depends, but never try to force it.

Domination with touch

This is a great way to start. In essence, you should tell the person you're going to take control. If they're good, you can blindfold, and you tell the person they're not allowed to move around, or pick a part that they're not allowed to move around.

They have to stay still, and then, you pleasure them. Do this however you want, whether it be feathers, fingernails, or whatever. You can use kissing, tickling, and force the other to stay still. You can even give oral sex into there, and you can try to see if they will come loose. A small paddle or a riding crop is a way to give punishment, and do make sure that you talk about impact play before you begin.

Foot Worship

Foot worship is something that actually can be quite sexy, and a fun way to spice up the bedroom. It's a subservient idea, and you can force your sub to lick your shoes, or your feet. You can keep the other away from you, and even kicking and prodding a little bit to goad the other is a great way to actually really show domination.

CBT bondage

This is a more extreme version, but you can use a cock ring to start out. You can then get different cock rings, and you can even invest in a "gates of hell" which is a device that has multiple cock rings.

You can even buy cages that wrap the genitals in there to prevent the man from getting hard. It's good if the man doesn't listen to directions, and you can even lock them. Of course, don't start out with this right away though, but work up to it.

Sissy play

Sissy play is essentially dressing a guy up in underwear for women, stockings, women's clothing, and garter belts. Some love it, and some hate it, but you can actually leverage this by rewarding or punishing the sub with it. You can put it in it, and even do their hair and makeup, and talk about how pretty, weak, or girly he is. Some like it as praise, so turn the comments to praise. If they hate it, spin it in a negative way too. It's something some guys really like, and it's a fun femdom idea.

Bondage Fun

Bondage is something that you may already be doing, but maybe you're on the other side this time, the one tying the man up. You can begin with binding wrists and ankles together so that you keep him bound. You can do regular cuffs, or even a hog tie if you feel like you want to stretch his body. Restraints for under the bed are also a great idea!

You can partner this with some gags to prevent the sub from speaking, blindfolds, spreads for the ankles that force the legs open, and even nipple clamps if he has sensitive nipples.

Tease for Success!

The last thing that we are going to discuss is teasing, and if you want to really take your femdom to the next level get that teasing in there. You can bind them and tell them not to touch you, get them hard, and then tease them, and you can essentially push them to the limits. You don't even need to use a lot of teasing for this, and if you want to really make him squirm, punish him with impact play.

It is a great way to show dominance, cause male submissives love to touch, but sometimes seeing their dommes masturbating in front of them can make them feel the ultimate tease.

Combining this with impact play is a great thing. You can tease a little bit, but then give a nice spanking with the hands, a cane or a flogger, or even use one of those fur paddles if they're not into really getting hit. Some guys are a bit weird about being hit, and it's something that you should make sure that you take some decent liberties with when you're trying it.

Now, with femdom, you can combine it with other fun little actions, including the roleplaying scenes that you may be interested in trying out. You can incorporate all of these into the scene, allowing for your sub to squirm in pleasure

Now as always, make sure that you do practice all of this with the safe precautions, and always have your safe words in play. You also need to have aftercare in place. Just because they're a big, strong man doesn't mean that they may not be shocked by this. In fact, they can be even more shocked than you expected because of the way this can be. It's a bit different to be on the other side of the coin, and if you're working with trying to get the man more comfortable with being a submissive, you need to keep the same rules that apply to when a female is the sub.

With femdom, remember that the rules are still there, regardless of who is on top. You could be a guy on bottom, or a girl on bottom. But, with our society normally forcing the gender roles that women are to be on bottom, and men on top, it's a new, refreshing way to truly understand and really experience the fun that is associated with sex and sexual freedom. If you've ever wanted to try femdom, you should definitely tell your man about it, and while it can be a bit scary, especially if you're someone who's conventionally a "good girl" it can be super liberating to have this happen, and if you're someone who enjoys the idea of dominating, even a little bit, then this could be something for you. So if anything, talk to your partner, and see if you want to try this.

Let's take a moment to talk about hard limits. Hard limits are something that subs put there that essentially are where they draw the line. But, some subs come into this dynamic trying to expand hard limits on their body. It's a bit strange to think of why a sub may do this, but we'll go over in this chapter why a sub may consider the idea of hard limits, and how a dom can expand on these hard limits without hurting the sub in any way. Remember, communication is the answer, and should be discussed before you start this.

The difference Between Hard and Soft Limits

Hard and soft limits are important to have in any BDSM scene. These are here for subs to explore different aspects of their sensuality in a safe manner, and essentially, it prevents the dom from doing things they aren't cool with. Lots of times, these limits involve giving up some form of control, and not make decisions, but the rules are in place, and they're there so that they won't do anything to hurt the sub. Essentially, they're guidelines on what's cool and what's not cool, and are respected.

Now there are two kinds, soft and hard. The difference is simple:

- Soft are limits that are cool with the sub, and essentially what they'll consent to. When you go into this, just assume that they're not okay with everything, but instead follow the limits that are put in with a contract before you begin. For example, nipple clamps, spanking, oral sex, and even bondage can be soft limits. The pain tolerance is also agreed upon too. Do you flog to bruise? Or do you want permanent scarring? These are what are agreed upon with the dom before you do anything.

- Hard limits are things that you just don't do. The doms have boundaries as well, and they can be things you're just not cool with.

- Requirements limits: they're usually not talked about in online discourse, but these are what a partner has to have, such as if a punishment hurts you to the point of crying, you need to implement aftercare.

Understanding these different limits is essentially to having a successful BDSM relationship with a sub.

What happens if not Respected?

Now sometimes if the limits aren't respected, it can mean a big issue. That's when it teeters into abuse. If for some reason it accidentally happens, the dom is warned never to do that again. They get off with a warning, but if it does happen again, the sub can stop the relationship.

Subs have power. They can terminate a contract at any time. That's what's so wild about it. The subs are the ones with power in hand, and that's something every dom needs to remember.

When to Expand

Limits are not something that stagnate however. Just because you may have disliked it in the past, doesn't mean that you may not always hate it. In fact, it can actually change over time. Sometimes, a sub might like something for a bit, but not for too long. It's important that as well, when doing scenes, you also aren't under the influence of drugs or alcohol, and you should be able to give your full consent to anything.

Usually though, knowing when you need to change is a personal thing. If you're discovering that you want to have more from your scenes, or your body feels like it's used to this, it might be time to start to expand on this.

Of course, this is a personal evaluation, and you should look at it in a way to challenge it and change the way that it is. If you're ready to try it, you should always let the other know, but you can always trial run it before it's put into a contract. If you like it, then you can change it.

Now for the dom, this really isn't your area of control. This is the sub's area of control, and if you think about it and feel like you've accomplished the limits and want to expand on it, it can be time to change. Sometimes, it will allow you to become a better slave or master. Of course, it's got to be a consensual agreement to change the limits.

With BDSM, it is all about exploring limits, and you're doing it with a person that you trust. With this, it's essentially learning how far you take these limits, and how far you can both go the distance together.

But of course, never cross the limits in a way that can hurt you. Pushing limits allows you to see the sphere of responsibility that you're able to handle, and can even be an endurance point. For example, maybe see how many spanks you can take, or also trying different play methods. Pushing limits should never be about endangering, and if you're going to practice something along the lines of edge play, always learn how to do it before you even think about trying it.

Some limits are strange too, in that one of them will send the sub into subspace, but another one causes you to have a panic attack. Limits do start to change over time.

For example, if you want to try something that you see at parties, you can do it in short spurts. Breath play is a good example, because you may have fear of it, or even health risks. But, if you do short sessions, it can actually send you into subspace if you end up liking it. Limits do change too, and you should be willing to accept change.

Communication About Limits

Now, with communicating these, you should always tell your dom whether or not you want something. You should tell the person not just that you won't allow you to do it, but the reasons why you may not like it. Simply saying no without basis can be a bit of a problem, since you may not even have any reasons for it, but may not want to try it due to potential societal conformity or other reasoning. You should have a reason for not doing it.

Sometimes if you're into the idea of threatening, the dom can threaten it if you like it, but doms always have at the forefront safety. They want to protect their toys, and you should always, as a sub, be crystal-clear about telling them the limits, and following the orders based on it.

Now, doms can take you a hair beyond the limits. You have these comfort zones right? Well, doms are there to expand upon them. It's definitely a good thing. In essence, as a dom, you want to challenge the soft limits. Not the hard ones, since if you do challenge that and things go sour, that's how it teeters on abuse. But, if you're a good match, it will almost feel like there aren't any limits to it, but if you're looking to explore, try to go for that. You should always make sure to take those soft limits, harness them, and make them stronger.

One thing that a sub should never say is that you have no limits. That's because you essentially are opening the door to many different elements and kinks that you may not be into. Are you into being branded? Do you want permanent scars? Do you want to sleep in a cage, with a small towel to keep you warm? Are you into being suffocated? If that's something that you don't want, you should always communicate it. There are limits to everything, and everyone should be communicative on the limits, expressing them, and doing what's right for you. Limits are there for our own personal safety and comfort, and probably one of the biggest mistakes, is to say that you have no limits. In a sense, everyone does, it may take a bit of time to fully explore the limits, but they exist.

You can always test hard limits over time, but remember, that the sub's the one who gets the final say in everything, and the dom should always follow the limits in their own way.

Another extreme form of play is mind fuck. Mind fuck and edge play are both more extreme uses of BDSM, and it's something that you should consider doing if you're very familiar with the partner, and you're both down to try it. Mind fucking is super powerful, since you're putting an extreme idea into the sub's head, instead of doing something that's safer, but it can bring fear play and adrenaline to a new level. It's a super powerful form of BDSM, and that, combined with edge play, is something that you could consider if that's something that you want to try. But, let's go over an example of this, and what you have to have before you even begin to try this.

So What is it?

Alright, let's take a scene where you've got the sub blindfolded, bound, and maybe naked in the shower. She may be cold, and you can tell her that you want to warm her up. You start to unzip your pants, and then, a warm feeling is on their chest. The sub thinks that it's urine, and you may continue on. You might start to start and stop this, and command the sub to open their mouth. The sub thinks that you're going to pee in her mouth, but then, the sub will realize that it's not piss, but maybe it's just hot water. The sub thinks this, and it brings forth a fear that starts to overtake them during scenes.

This is essentially psychological manipulation. It can temporarily confuse, destabilize, and manipulate the partner, and in essence the reason for this is to release endorphins and adrenaline, and it can give a very natural high to it.

So is it Safe?

It is, but you have to remember that the mind is a key element to BDSM. Trust is a huge factor in this, and mind fucks can actually be very dangerous if you're nor familiar with the person. If you're going to try a mind fuck, you should make sure that you've played with this partner for a long time before you even think about attempting it, since trust is a super valuable thing, and the quickest way to scare off a newbie, or scar them from ever trying a BDSM scene is to do this at the wrong time. It also makes you look bad too. Fear doesn't usually come into play unless something is dramatic, so make sure that the bottom is fine with you doing this, and trusts you. Remember that if you're worried you'll hurt them, then don't do it. Also, make sure you know they know that you're not being serious, since this could actually turn violent if the person thinks that you're serious.

Other Examples

You can even go more extreme with this. For example, let's say that you have the sub over there, spanking and then jokingly say you have a power drill near the back of the car. The sub may be blindfolded, and they hear the power drill. This can cause the sub to freak out, and you then stop the scene.

You can even use threaten of castration, and even include medical knives and tools, and you can even clamp their testicles in a cage and even add some ice to it to numb the person down. You can make then pretend that you're doing this. However, this is something that you shouldn't even try if you don't already know how to initiate scenes, since the clamps can be hard to control in terms of variables. But, when you're done, you take off the clamps, and then the blood will come back, and if you blindfold the man, you can even make it seem like they actually did get castrated.

Even something as a butcher knife can be used to threaten. You can pretend that you're getting something from the kitchen, make them see the butcher knife, and then bring "it" to their throat. Course it's not a butcher knife, it's the side that's not slotted on a butter knife. If it's cold and steel, they won't know the difference, don't actually use the butcher knife.

With this though, need to have a few key ingredients before you attempt this.

The key Ingredients.

There are a few ingredients you should always have before you try something like this, and they are as follows:

- Trust: for the love of god, if you're going to go through with this, do have trust. If not, you may have a lawsuit come up shortly after.

- Communication: You should vocalize and talk to the sub, tell them how it feels, and you can essentially fan the fire. Subs love details, and if you can do it without too many details, it gives a thrill without the brain actually thinking it's happening.

- Be ready to brainstorm: you want to essentially make safer ways than the real thing.

- Blindfolds and restraints are key: adding this will make the experience better, and it can help improve the actual mind fuck on the dominant's end.

- Consent: you need to have consent that it's okay to push the boundaries. Make sure that you discuss this and make sure that they're cool with exploring this, so long as they are interested, and you don't go towards hard limits and make sure they know safe words too.

- Get info: you can build the perfect mind fuck scene by playing into fears and fantasies, such as maybe the fantasy of a gangbang, being abducted, or even interrogation. Listen to what they say, and do cater to these along with personal limits. You can also play into fear as well, or maybe even consensual non consent play. Once you do have the consent and the fears at hand, find you what turns them on.

- Planting seeds: you can even plant these seeds by telling your partner of the fucked up things you want to do, or even what to do when you're in bed together. Push the boundaries and threaten them as well, and try to push them into real life.

Now with these scenes, you want to make sure that you plan how to set it up, including what senses you want to play with, and anything that you should avoid since it might cause them to be triggered in a way they shouldn't be triggered.

If you have props, introduce them to the partner, since it will get them to be nervous.

If there are others involved, make sure they know the scene, and any triggers that you want, and they know how to respond, in case if the partner figures it out, and how they should respond in an emergency.

Now, when you do reveal this, you want to show them that what they experienced wasn't actually the reality they thought. This can be a bit jarring and shocking, which is why you NEED aftercare. Mind fucks can in fact, fuck a person up, and you shouldn't participate with this unless you're ready to face and handle the fallout. You should understand that it does take time to reform the connection that was there. You should always make sure that they get aftercare, since mind fuck is an atypical scene, and the person may need to spend hours or days near you, and you need to reassure them that you'd never actually harm them. You should discuss the scene and talk about the experience too. It's a very in-depth process, but it actually can be a fun experience. If you do try a mind fuck, always do it with someone you trust, make sure that safety is at the forefront, and you do cater to the person's fantasies, limits, and the like.

Sometimes, you want something a bit more. This does tend to happen. If you've ever been interested in creating bigger scenes, or more in-depth ones, or even relationships, you should know about how to negotiate them with the dom. Of course, with BDSM, you're always growing, and it's totally fine to negotiate for different elements. Here is how you can, and some of the different aspects to consider.

Knowing you Want It

You first have to know that you want it. For example, maybe you've wanted to try medical play, and you've thought about negotiating that scene. Perhaps you have a few triggers, but you still feel the urge to try it. Or maybe you've been with a dom for a while and you want to try a mind fuck. This is something you're going to need to make sure that you know that you want.

The problem, is that sometimes fantasies get in the way of reality. Negotiating scenes can often cause you to imagine either the worst, or the best. If that's the case, you should definitely make sure that you know that you want it, and that you're with a dom that you can trust. If you're starting out a relationship with a dom, don't go into edgeplay right away, but if you're curious about doing things you should definitely make sure that you talk about it with the dom when you're ready.

Negotiating Scenes

For scene negotiation, you want to focus on your activities and interactions. You should do this well before the actual scene itself, and if you're working with others at a party or event, you should always make sure that the needs, wants, limits, concerns, and whatever are known. Now, you can do this on the spot too, and if you're having a play date, you can sit around and discuss the scene over tea or coffee, and if you want to negotiate a bigger scene here, you can go for it.

You should keep the conversation around the following elements.

- What you want from it

- Limits that are there

- Any experience prior to this regarding the play

- Health conditions that should be known

- Various medications that you have on hand just in case

- Any triggers that should be known

- Aftercare

- Preventative maintenance that might be needed

Now, the general rule is that the more intense the scene, the more aftercare that you'll need. Usually, if you're doing this at the party, you'll feel the drop after that, which is the psychological lowering of the intensity, and all of your hormone normalizing once again. You should make sure that bodily, along with mental aftercare is at the forefront.

Lots of times, you want to make sure that the hard limits are defined, and never implied. No and yes are concrete terms, and the hard limits are never negotiated. Wants should be at the helm as well, since this is something that you should be going for.

If you're picking up scenes at events and parties, you should always be absolute and clear, so that there aren't any misunderstandings, and issues with a public scene. It also does make the Dungeon Masters if they're on duty at a party able to judge whether a scene is good or bad, or if there is danger and needs to be stopped.

Mental afflictions should be discussed too, such as how you respond to play, whether it's through disassociation, verbalizing, time dilation, and how check-ins should be good. Its also something important to discuss the non-verbal cues that may be needed in case things end up going sour in the process. You should make sure that you don't have wiggle room, and you're not wishy washy about this. You should make sure that the more complex the scene, the more chance for chaos, so always be on your toes with this.

Always Focus on Consent, and Any Medical Concerns

You should always, ALWAYS focus on making sure that consent is at the forefront. Always make sure the sub is cool with whatever you're doing before you do it. When forming the contract for different scenes, or scenes at a dungeon, you should always make sure everyone is in agreement.

You should also make sure with this that the safe words are there. Usually, the stoplight system is used, such as green meaning that is good, yellow means you may need to slow down, and red is stopping. However, that can be a bit of a problem since yellow can mean different things. Lots of times, the yellow might mean to lighten up, but the top may not know that, so sometimes it's best to make sure that you have these safe words established, and if you use a particular safe word, it's known by the other party members and the dom themselves, and they stop the scene.

Then there is the medical aspect of it. When negotiating for a bigger scene, you should always make sure that any surgery issues with joints, or known medical conditions are known. But you should also know if they have asthma, allergies, blood sugar issues, and the like are often catered to. Rope may have natural fibers, and the toys may have silicone in them, which may cause an allergic reaction. So always make sure that you talk about this with the dom, and let them know of medical concerns beforehand.

Negotiating Relationships

This is something you should concern yourself with if you're going to be with a dom for a while. This should be discussed between both of you, and it involves the way the relationship is, power dynamics, responsibilities and the roles of it, and any goals in the long term. For example, you should agree that the evolution is a shared one, and you both have an agreed-upon role. You can also agree that you may have a triad that you use for occasional open use and play. The limits in relationships do have some wiggle room, a bit more than in negotiating scenes, but remember that you should make sure to group the hard limits, soft limits, and anything in between as well.

Wants can also have similar types of elements in terms of what you want, and can be the primary aspect of the relationship. Lots of times, with relationships, you should always make sure that you know this, and keep it as a primary element, such as maybe a power exchange and kink, and keep that dynamic at the helm while trying to strengthen it, while also keeping the limits honored, and working to slowly remove all of the limits so that the sub can reach a new level. Essentially, if you're going into this for the long haul, you should always have this conversation on what you want to get out of this, how it can be achieved, and any limits that may come about because of this.

With negotiating scenes you should always do what works for you. Negotiation is a big part of BDSM, especially for talking about going about improving the limits, so definitely ensure that you have all of this in mind when you're doing what you feel is right for yourself and your partner.

When being a sub, sometimes, it's quite hard to sometimes get into it. It can be different for you, and sometimes, you want to be a better sub to your partner. Being on the bottom can be a bit different, and sometimes being a submissive can be a completely different situation. But, if you're looking to be a better one, do remember these tips.

You Control it All

At the end of the day, you know who has all of the control? You. You're the one who gets to control what will happen. It's a consensual exchange of power, and you're agreeing to different factors. You are choosing to surrender, and the choice is yours, and from this moment forward, with mutual agreement, the choices are essentially yours, not just his. You sat down and made an agreement, right? Well there you go, you can choose that, and if you need to take responsibility for something, do so.

Give in Sometimes

Sometimes, when you're considering getting into this, the idea of relinquishing control is a bit strange. Sometimes, you're so used to telling others what to do, arguing and being in control, that this can be a jarring experience. You may have so many reasons why you don't want to do it, that you're giving yourself so many excuses.

One of the cool things about submission is that you're going to actually submit and fully give in. Letting go, letting domination take over, and the thrill of it isn't necessarily a bad thing.

It's hard for those who constantly live in a state where they need to be on top to submit. Do you have a life where you're always focused on being the one in control? Well, it can be a bit hard for you to really let go. Getting that trust built is something that you'll need to do. Learn to listen, and accept the guidance. If you have something that does go against the grain, talk to them about it, and learn to express yourself.

Engage in Subspace

Subspace goes along with letting go. When you're in a scene, you want to achieve subspace, which is the total lack of control on your own end, a space where the dom is fully on control of your body. It's a scary thing to do, and sometimes, it takes trust. If you don't have it yet, this can be a hard situation for you to overcome, but if you learn to acknowledge that you don't always have to be in control, you'll be amazed at the difference.

Trust your Dom

Trust is a major part of this. If you don't have it with your dom, you're going to have a bad time. If you're worried about something, talk to the dom, and make sure that he respects your boundaries. If he can actually help you become a better version of yourself, and actively take control, then there is nothing wrong with letting go a little bit, and trying something new. It's something that you will want to remember.

Remember as well, that doms want to be the best caretaker and dominant to you. They consider you a plaything at times, yes, but they actively do want to take care of you despite being regarded as a plaything. They ultimately want to see you grow.

If your dominant doesn't want to see you get better, that is a red flag, and something that you'll need to watch out for. The dominant works towards the goals that you set forward.

Maintain your goals

With many BDSM relationships, goals are what are at the forefront. If you don't have goals put in already, it's imperative that you do something about it. Make sure that you have a set, delineated goal that you both want to work towards. Try to ensure that you guys are on the same page.

If the goal changes at any instance, let your dom know about it. They're here to help you maintain these goals, so if they're not doing that, then something needs to give, and you need to make sure you communicate any problems as well.

Have Self-Respect

Self-respect goes a long way, and the best relationships in this light are based on it, even if it does mean humiliation. You both respect each other, but there is an even bigger element to it: respecting yourself.

You should definitely remember that you do have power, and that you have to have power before you end up giving it away. You should make sure that you can control yourself too. While it's great to just sit there and abandon all control whatsoever, you do need to make sure that you know exactly what the safety switch is, that you're willing to say a safe word if it gets too heavy.

Lots of times, people may run into BDSM because they have no self-respect for themselves, and they think that maybe they can get over the self-degradation that they have. If you feel like this is describing you, chances are you need to sit back and learn to respect yourself, and not let anyone damage your health period, whether it be emotional, financial, or even psychical health. While yes, your dominant should regard you as someone to cherish, don't think that you're off the hook when it comes to taking care of yourself. If you're unable to take care of yourself, you may lose the chance to give anything to the dom period, so if you're in trouble, speak up. The dominant needs to know if you're okay, and it's a super responsible thing. If your dominant doesn't listen and cater to the needs, you'll know right then and there that they may not care about you, and it's an abusive relationship.

Do Learn Generosity

Just because you're a sub, doesn't mean that you're a passive period. Submission should be open and receptive, and the pleasure should happen in both ways.

Dominants like submissives that learn to be a giving and generous period. For example, learn to observe your dom, and open up your heart and eyes, and actually listen to what he likes, and what he dislikes, and from there, follow that and become a generous period. Give them the generosity that they deserve. The dominant will give you the same back. The best dominants out there do know what you need more than you may know, and the same goes on the other side of the coin.

When it comes to criticizing, you should be against doing it, and sometimes, be careful with humor, because sometimes, humor may have some criticisms attached to it. Being a critical person can actually be very toxic, and it's not something others want to hear. Instead of evaluating and making him feel bad for what he's doing, tell him what he's doing right, and actually give gentle reminders and honor the man.

Do be a nice person. Remember, just because you're a submissive doesn't mean that you can't be nice. You may be a bratty sub in the bedroom, but that doesn't mean that you should be rude in general. If you want him to forgive your mistakes, forgive his. It does happen, none of us are perfect, and this especially goes if one of you make mistakes at this point. Little bit of compassion and kindness can go a long way, and since they don't cost much to give, what's so bad about that?

Relax and have Fun

Some of the greatest pleasure isn't something sexual, but instead, you can actually engage in laughter. It's something that you should consider. D/s relationships are not some sort of serious and melodramatic thing, but it's okay to be silly and funny, but definitely be sensitive on the timing and make sure that you're kind with it. Being able to laugh sometimes is a good thing.

These will help you be a better submissive, and it can make a world of a difference when working with a dom sometimes.

Chapter 9: How to Help a Sub if they're going downhill

Sometimes there is the situation where the dom tries to do everything in their power to help the submissive, but maybe there is a situation where the submissive is just going downhill, and it's affecting the dynamic. How can you rectify this? What is the best way to fix a sub that is just having issues in life? Well, let's discuss this.

You may Be the Dominant, but you're Shaping the Submissive

You may wonder why you'd even consider trying to help a submissive if they're going downhill, but let's take a moment to discuss the problems that come with submissives at times.

Submissives aren't perfect. They have their faults. Lots of times, they try to get themselves together, and you enter into a contractual agreement to help the other out. But, maybe the submissive hit a wall, and they're struggling with trying to overcome it. Instead of having them go through it alone, you've got to step in.

Dominants should care for their submissives. This includes actually shaping them into better people. It doesn't take much to really help your submissive, and sometimes, it can really change them for the better. If you've ever wondered just how much of an impact you make as a dom, you should look at the contract. You're both looking to get better, so it's obvious that you're a focal part of this.

Talk to Them

The first thing, is to observe. Look at them, and if you notice that something is wrong, talk to them. Perhaps when you're both sitting down to discuss a scene, or after a scene, you talk to them. Remember, you're in a relationship with them, so you should go and talk with them about the problem.

They may be a bit against discussing it, but let them know that they're not in trouble or anything, but instead, you're just trying to help them out. You'd be amazed what the difference will make if you do it like this.

Find out what the root of the issue is

When you're talking to them, you want to go for the meat of the problem, why they're suffering from this. Subs may tend to beat around the bush if this is a major concern, but you as a dom should try to steer the conversation towards a better understanding of the problem. If the sub has an issue with say, maybe school or work, find out what the root of the issue is. Remember, you want to assure them that they don't have to do this alone.

Lots of times, subs may not even have the ability to tell others of the issue, and they see it as a blessing to have that extra being around to help them out. You want to show them that you care a lot about them, but you also don't want to be the one to make their decisions. Get to the root, but also don't be rude about it, but instead, you should work on this together.

Work to Put a Plan together

You two should sit down and make a plan. Maybe start with the problem, the possible solutions for it, and what can be accomplished right away. You should hold the sub accountable for any problems that come about, but also remember, that you're the dom, so you should be the one to control if there is something there. Lots of times, subs are willing to listen, and if there is a disagreement, you two can easily talk it out. It's quite nice, and it's something that you'd be amazed can make a difference and work. If you've ever been interested in helping your sub, sometimes this little discussion can go a long way. Actually put a concrete plan together. If it does end up being an addiction or something, try to get them the help that they need. You as a dom are responsible for your toy, so make sure not to forget that.

Intervene if you Need to

Now, if the sub responds well to this help, chances are, the two of you can get through the problem together, and actively work out a solution. But if there is the off chance that the sub managed to go downhill again, or you notice that they're not actively taking care of themselves, you'll need to intervene.

Remember, you're doing this to help the sub. While it may be a bit of tough love, it is tough love. When a sub goes downhill, they sometimes need all of the help that they can get, and all of the assistance that's possible. It's up to you as the dominant to realize this, and to make sure that if possible, you stop the sub from doing something that they'll later regret. It may be a small thing now, but it can make a huge difference when it comes to actively taking control and helping the sub to get better in life.

If they're Doing themselves in Too Much, you can Disengage

Unfortunately, there are the moments when the sub just isn't listening, that you've done all that you can, but they're refusing to agree to terms. Perhaps you put in the contract that you don't want them to drink too much, and you catch them deep in a bottle of wine. You tell them not to do it, and they don't listen, despite multiple reprimands. You can only do so much, and sometimes, the sub may need to realize how bad they are before they can help themselves.

Remember, you can disengage from a contract at any time. If it's too much to bear, you can always tell the sub that you're not fit to be the dom anymore, that you can't take care of that need. This can be a bit of an embarrassing instance, but sometimes, it's better to be honest with yourself. If your sub refuses to get help, it can be trying on you, so definitely make sure that you take your time, and you make sure that you do what you feel is right.

With a sub, sometimes they fall off the beaten path, and you as a dom need to realize this. If you're not careful, it can be a real problem. Do make sure that you take care of your sub, and help them accordingly when something goes wrong.

Chapter 10: How to Handle Multiple Subs

Sometimes, adding a second dominant and submissive might be an action people take. Some don't like it because there is the universal acceptance of a singular dom and multiple submissives. It's an esteem that can sometimes be there, and some people see it as enticing. Sometimes, new dominants go through a phase that involves different judgments and choices that might be made.

Sometimes, new submissives discover that they have this identity through the internet. Some submissives are married, and sometimes, it's not always a happy one. Sometimes the excitement isn't there, and they're terse and not excited. A lot of submissives have this loss of hope happen when they're not taken care of, and lots of times, their personal appearance and personality starts to diminish, and over time, the submissives feel like there is a gnawing hole in them, and they feel this ache, and lots of times, if the goals aren't met, the sensation is gone.

Sometimes though, having multiple dominants can often start to change the way a submissive feels. That's cause, if the relationships are online, they have multiple ones that are on-call, and often, it's a way to evade the idea of long-term commitment, since often some submissives don't actively take control.

Sometimes, a submissive can have multiple dominants if they feel like this is the right choice. It might be something for you, if you have something that your current dom can't have. However, it's often something that isn't really actively pursued.

With a multiple dominant relationship, remember that each dominant has different contracts, and you should respect each of them. It's a way to seek out fulfillment as a sub. If you as a dominant don't like it, always communicate to your sub, and learn to understand their feelings, and get them to understand your accordingly.

What About Submissives

Sometimes, dominants get this idea that they want to add a bunch of submissives to their relationships, because of childhood fantasies, and being able to live out the harem fantasy that they may have. Lots of times though, it can be a big problem.

BDSM communities tend to almost be like opening up your presents on Christmas morning. It's like you're given all of these new opportunities, but often, it might be a bit overwhelming, and sometimes, people don't realize the ramifications of actions.

If you choose to add a submissive, do actually think of the ramifications, including jealousy, and possible damage that this might incur. It can actually be a good thing if you've communicated it, but lots of times people don't look at the full spectrum of the picture.

Many times, people discover this through the internet, via spicing up their marriage or relationships. It can be quite hard because you're already ingrained in the responses, habits, and attitudes, and being able to explore these new possibility can change the way a person is.

Many tend to flock towards this because of how different that they're treated, and often, being involved with this are different than how they're treated in their current real-life relationships. They often don't think that there is anything bad about a second submissive.

The problem is though, that a second submissive creates a problem. Usually, the submissive feels like they're pressured into doing this, or they will have their worlds disputed. This is because the relationship has it already built, and the introduction of another person as an addition can create instability in the relationship. The submissive might conceptualize that the person who is entering will make them feel abandoned, lost, unstable, and they will feel like their family structure is lost, and they lose their social status, and it might make them feel shameful. Often these feelings are stuffed inside. This is very true if the submissive is trying to live up to the ideal, and they have this relationship already extremely solidified.

The dominant might not even realize this, since they're looking at their own lust and are blinded by this that they don't see the implications. Many times, the dominants think that they can handle all the needs of the submissives.

If you're going to add a submissive, here is what you have to remember: you need to handle all of their needs and wants, and you want to make sure your submissives don't get upset. You want to make sure that they have the strong personal attention that you can give them, and the dominant needs to realize that it does impact the ties. It might be cool to have another submissive, but it's definitely a bit of a forcible situation.

Don't forcibly do this. If you do choose to do this, we'll tell you how you can incorporate this below.

Tips on how to

The best way to do this is to make sure that you do the following;

- Talk to the primary sub

- Get an agreement on this, and make sure that it's within their desires

- If they don't want it, don't do it

- If you force it, you'll upset everyone

- When you do it, remember you're handling two people

- Make sure that they can trust you on this

- Always consider the needs and requirements that each of them have

- Always make sure to communicate, because being able to do so is crucial with this type of addition

Adding submissive is something that you should consider if you want it. You both want to have it though. Remember that these are contractual relationships, so you need to be accepting of whatever comes your way. Always do consider this, and make sure you're smart about it whenever this does become a situation. Do respect the wishes of your sub, and you'll be able to make them happy as well, and always focus on the primary sub's own feelings. It might seem like a good idea, but not everyone can handle it, and it's something that you need to remember.

Chapter 11: Caning and Other Hard Impact Play Ideas

We have talked about spanking and other impact play, but let's talk about some of the more extreme forms of this. Caning is a big one, and we'll go over a couple of these. Impact play is a huge part of kink, since many times, people love spankings, but impact play has a lot of different types, all which do involve hitting the area.

Lots of people love it because of pain, but some have different pain tolerances. If you've tried spankings and floggings and want something a bit more, then it's time for you to maybe try to explore these more extreme limits.

These can be used for discipline, punishment and funishment, and humiliation. Discipline like whipping and flogging can be used as a form of an endurance test. With some power exchange relationships, these are used to punish bad behavior, broken rules, being sassy, or whatever, but some like to have it as a form of funishment, where it's not meant to be disrespectful, but for fun. For humiliations, it can be also used to humiliate the person that doesn't like getting them. Slapping in the face is another one, since it's personal, but some get off to it. It can trigger bad memories though, so be careful when this is used in a more humiliating sort of mindset.

So what are some of the more extreme ones? Well, let's explore them.

Whipping

Whipping is essentially like flogging, but there is much more impact. That's because usually these are made with leather, and since most of the force is compacted into one singular tail, hitting the person does inflict deeper welts. These can even draw blood.

With whipping, always practice on a pillow, bench, or something other than a person until you're used to it.

The one most used is a bull whip, which is used around a person's body and snakes around when it impacts. You should definitely make sure you practice and have a lot of experience before you use this type of whip, since it does endanger the vital organs potentially. There is the dragon's tail though which is easier for beginners, the stock whip that creates a good cracking sounds due to the long handle, and if you fish it's like a fishing rod, a quirt which is like the stock whip but is more forked, and there is the snake whip, which snakes around like a snake.

Now, how does this play in the ouch factor? The answer, is a nice little sting. But, remember that the amount of pain, and the type of pain you feel is really dependent on the hardness and the fastness of the whip striking the body, and the result of it. You should always have safe words in play, but whipping especially since this can draw blood, cut up the skin, and can hurt the person. And always make sure that you perform aftercare after using one of these.

Caning

Now caning is one of those types of impact play that people either love, or they hate. Some want the cane, some hate the cane. Some doms love it, some not so much, the sub either begs or cries for it.

Caning in essence is striking with a rod that's long and cylindrical that strike the body in areas that have a large muscle, but you can use it on the feet and some other areas of the body itself.

What can they be made of? Well, you can get one that's made out of wood, bamboo, plastic, or whatever. These are anywhere from 12-18 inches to even a few feet in length.

Now, the characteristic of this one, is the ability to localize the sensation, impact, and the pain that you feel. It almost feels like your skin is ripping in impact. However, unlike flogging where it can be on a superficial area, this has the sensation localized to a specific location on the body. It typically happens on the bottom, and it can leave marks and bruises behind without as many forces and strikes.

Now, if the person you're caning is sensitive to pain, mix in the sensations, and then give a few quick strikes. Many attribute caning to exclamation points in a sense. If you do enjoy the sensation, start slow and build up the strikes. A little bit of this does go a long way, so make sure you're not going too hog wild with the cane and hitting the person with it a hundred times, but instead a few strikes here and there.

Slapping and Punching

This is one that's not discussed often is slapping and punching. This is a form of impact play, but often less common since it does have a stigma around it, since people are taught not to do this. Slapping is open-handed, while punching is a closed hand. Now, you should make sure they're not done with anger imbued, or without consent. Always talk to the submissive or dominant before you try this.

Masochists and submissives that like rough sex for example, do enjoy this. Some people like the idea of a small slap being administered to get the partner to look at you or their attention. Lots of times, sometimes when a person is slapped during sex, the body clenches around the cock, and that's something that people like. It also may send some subs into subspace due to the impact it bestows to you.

Whether you're slapping or punching, you should try to get some cues into place. For example, with slapping, touching the cheek is a signal that you're about to slap the person. Once you slap them once, relax your hand. For the sub, you should relax the jaw when you notice that you may get slapped, since a clenched jaw hurts and can rattle the teeth, which isn't fun.

With punching, never do it in the facial area. You also never want to hit the partner with the knuckles, but instead, use the flat area of the fist, and only strike the larger muscle groups so that you don't actively hurt the person. don't punch the rib area for example. You usually can slap and punch the partner in both of the areas that are okay to slap.

You should slap and punch along the following area:

- Near the back and shoulders area next to the spine, but never on the spine, cause that can cause fractures and other damages

- Across the butt, a place with a lot of muscle and fatty tissue

- On the thighs, whether back or front, again lots of muscles and tissues that you won't have to worry about hurting

- The arm, ideally the upper area where there is more flesh

- The calves, but again only the back

- Chest area, but above the breasts, but not near the collarbone. However, some people like to be slapped and punched in the breasts, but do be careful

You'll definitely be likely to punch someone with their back over their butt, and make sure that when you do this, you listen to both reactions and cues. If you get punched, make sure that if it does end up with you getting hurt, tell your partner about it. If the pain isn't good, don't hold back. You should make sure that you don't feel the knuckles when you do, because that hurts.

Also, avoid the stomach and sides. That's where internal organs, and if you're worried about being too forceful, always make sure that you practice before using your hand in that manner.

With all types of impact play, always make sure that you provide aftercare after all of that. This can hurt, and you may have some bruising and welts from it. The sub may have entered subspace and may not be lucid as well. There might also be emotions that can happen here. Always get them water, blanket, and talking to them if they can talk. Also, do help cover any wounds and take care of bruising. You should also wait until they can talk first, and make sure that as a dom, you check with the sub a few hours after the scene is done so that they're okay physically and mentally.

Chapter 12: Choking and Cautions with it

Choking is a type of edge play that some people do enjoy, since the practice does constrict and can block off a person's air supply. This can cause permanent and severe damage to the larynx and carotid arteries, and if you're not careful, it can cause heart attacks and death. There isn't a safe way to choke someone, but it does cause a sexual high in a sense.

Why some enjoy it?

There are a few reasons some may enjoy choking, and they are as follows:

- It reinforces dominance over the submissive

- Some enjoy the sexual high from it

- Some like the lightheaded nature of it.

Now, because of that, as long as you're careful, you definitely can do this.

The Best way to do it?

The best way to choke someone is by putting pressure on the carotid arteries that are on the sides of the neck. don't put it on the windpipe directly, and that's because the arteries that are here have a lot of oxygen-rich blood, and when they're compressed, the brain is losing oxygen, and instead they're replacing it with carbon dioxide, which is why when you choke like this, you create a euphoric and giddy feeling that does cause the senses to be heightened. You can cause the sensations to last for about 3-5 seconds, but then, the person that is choked may end up passing out.

Now, if you do this, you should definitely never do this alone. The person that is choking the other should know CPR, and choking someone until they pass out is something that shouldn't be done with someone who isn't experienced in the element of choking.

Communication before, during, and after choking is a very crucial part of this. That's because you want to make sure that all communication is done, and if the person can't actually do this, then you should have a signal system in order to make sure that you have a good feel for this.

What to be careful with trying: Asphyxiophilia

This in essence is literally controlling the breath with sexual stimulation as the intent. The oxygen in this is reduced, and it heightens the orgasm.

When it's performed with someone, it's known as erotic asphyxiation, but when it's alone when masturbating, it's autoerotic. This is essentially breath control play or scarfing, and the person doing it is known as a gasper.

Now, you can practice this with hanging, plastic bag suffocation, self-strangulation with volatile solvent or gas, chest compression, or even a combination of all of these. Oxygen is suddenly lost to the brain, and then it causes a super rush to the body. The euphoria creates a state that's called hypoxia, which causes extreme sexual stimulation, and orgasm.

This is super additive, and super powerful, as strong of an addiction as cocaine, and it's like a euphoric feeling that some can experience when climbing high altitudes.

Now, doing this is incredibly dangerous, and you shouldn't try this. That's because these tend to cause about 200–1000 deaths each year, and they're even mistaken for suicide. Deaths can happen from the loss of consciousness that comes from this, and loss of control from the strangulation. Lots of times, this is a very risky behavior, and something that you should avoid trying period.

Breath Control Play

Breath control play is the use of choking or other forms with a partner, and when the brain is deprived of oxygen, creates a high. It's a deadly and dangerous activity, so you need to be super careful. If you do this, you should use safe words, gestures, and never use belts, ropes, cords, hanging, or pressures of an extreme sense to cut off the oxygen. You should, if you're going to do this, be in complete communication with your partner if you even dare to try this.

How much pressure?

So what is the best amount of pressure? The answer, is essentially up to you. The best way to do it, is to squeeze and release. Put the thumb and fingers there, count for a second, and then release. Do it to yourself, and continue until you understand.

Now, remember orgasms don't occur when the blood isn't flowing, and only happens when blood is present. There are people that do it to the point of being unconscious, and it's not something that amateurs should even try, and it may not be for everyone, so definitely make sure that you are doing it almost like how a lion holds their cubs by the scruff of the neck. Practice, and then work your way up to it.

A couple Techniques

We already talked about the pressure to the side of the neck, but make sure that you don't let body weight pressure grow there.

You can use the jawline to create a helplessness and not in control, and even the idea of hands on the neck gets her off, and you don't even have to apply pressure. Cupping the neck and putting it on the side of the neck is a good start.

You can also give the feeling of choking with hands, and don't apply pressure to the sides of the neck whatsoever. These are all good techniques to start with, and some that you can try to really make your partner scream.

Dos and Don'ts

There are a few dos and don'ts that can work with this, and they are as follows:

- Do assert dominance

- Do maintain eye contact

- Do stop thrusting and ask if they want it harder, and ask

- Do dirty talk when she's close

- Do try to get her to beg

- Don't apply pressure on the windpipe

- Don't pull the neck up

- Don't use grip to move the body around, but instead use hips, legs, and the thighs to pull the other down

- Don't be unaware of surroundings

- Don't try to choke someone when you're drunk, n medications, or if they're high

With choking, you should always make sure that you're not actively intending to choke to restrict their breathing, and always do it when they ask for it, since that is consensual, and they like the feeling. If you feel like it's wrong, chances are that it's wrong, but when you do it right, you're doing it right, since it does give an amazing feeling. If you're doubtful of your technique, you should always take it slow, and make sure to put your hands there without applying pressure, and then work your way up to what you really want from this.

One area of BDSM some people want to try is blood play. This usually involves blood, cutting, and knives. While this may be something that might be a bit much for the average vanilla person, if you've ever been immersed in the lifestyle and wanted to try it, you definitely will want to read up on not just how you do it, and how to do it safely.

Knife play, or blood play does have intrinsic danger to it. Remember, you're working with blood, so you definitely will want to make sure that you're safe. We will go over why people do this, and what safety precautions you want to have in mind before you do this.

So What is it?

Blood play is a form of edge play, which is essentially extreme BDSM that's often considered taboo. It involves cutting parts of the body to let blood come out. We may think of blood in a vanilla way, such as period sex and the like, but this involves a much more in-depth look to it, and often, it involves directly cutting the area, and it does involve smearing blood on the body, objects, drinking it, or the sensation and image of blood letting.

Why People Like this

So why would people be into this? Well, some like it as a symbolic image, and some people use the blood of the partner as a necklace, and it's something that some people see as a form of dominance.

It also plays into the primal instincts, along with intimacy. Blood is red, and often that symbolizes passion and trust. You don't do blood play with just any old person, and we'll get into why and the obvious safety precautions that are associated with it.

Some people also like this because of the pain associated with it. Lots of times, even those small cuts can curt, and lots of times, it does involve the element of trust, since you're giving your body and trust to someone that could put you into a life or death situation. It also is cathartic, and some people who are on the dominating end of this like to see the blood come out of the areas they inflict pain on.

Some also use this for touching on issues of self-harm. If there is trauma related to that, sometimes it can be cathartic in a sense, but it's often a very rare circumstance. They're not necessarily driven by harmful urges, but often it's the fetish of blood.

Is this Common?

The truth is, it's actually not that common. It's hard to say that many actually do this, but it's pretty obvious that this type of edge play isn't as popular. The popular reddits only have about 109 different subscribers, and the subreddits only about 13 of them.

It's also something that many people may not talk about period since there are extreme dangers that are associated with it. We will go over some of the risks later on, and why you have to be very careful. It's a fetish that involves a lot of responsibility. You never want to cut any of the vital arteries, or else you're going to end up on a nice trip to the hospital. It's an off-the-beaten path that many times, people are a bit scared to take. But, it's encouraged that if you do try this, you do it first in practice before you ever touch a live body.

So What's the Risk

Well there are a few major risks that you're going to want to be careful about when it comes to this type of edge play.

The first, and most obvious, is accidentally drawing too much blood. If you do, this brings about risk of death, and other such problems. Obviously, if you're going to do this, you need to make sure that you look at your sub, and you try to make sure you keep in communication at all times. This is probably your most obvious risk.

But, let's also talk about what blood contains. The extreme danger of infections from cuts is a major part of this, and also, STIs can be transmitted if you do exchange blood with your partner. You should never exchange it with a partner, because you could catch blood borne illnesses that the other person has. If you do however in the off chance exchange this, do make sure that you get tested for HIV before you even think about doing this.

Some Safety Precautions

There are many safety precautions that we will discuss here, and various elements you should always make sure that you keep in mind. Obviously, do everything known to RACK standards, which means risk aware consensual kink. You need to be consensual, and be aware of the risks. We will go over other different elements you should always have in mind.

Some of these are as follows:

- Always sterilize your instruments
- Test for infectious diseases

- Always take an STD test before you do this

- Only get blood from the meatier areas of the body

- Avoid drawing from major veins and Artie res

- Pick a safe word for both of you if you need it

- Have a safety kit ready that's got antiseptic, Band-Aids, ice packs, gauze, and other items you may need

- Keep some aftercare items nearby, since this can be a bit shocking

- Have a phone on hand if you need to call 911

Now, if you're wondering about maybe doing this, there are a few types of people that shouldn't engage in blood play, and they are as follows:

- Those on blood thinners

- Those who have issues with clotting blood

- Those that sett cutting as a trigger

- Those that can't handle blood

If you do this with those problems, it is possible that you may hurt yourself. Also never do this when angry, since this does fall under abuse.

The best places to cut, are the upper thighs, buttocks, forearms, and that's it. Avoid the backs of calves, the backs, and chest area. As for bad zones, avoid the torso and areas below the knee. The three critical areas to avoid are the area near the Achilles tendon, back of knee, back of wrist, armpit and upper forearm area, near the genitals, and neck. These are danger zones, and you may cut either a vein or a tendon, which is incredibly dangerous.

You need to be careful, since this is one of those areas that can potentially be life-threatening.

Now, if you want to do blood play, you want to cut deep enough to draw blood. Usually, if you don't want to do that, you usually are doing knife play, which involves cutting a couple layers with the blade in a gentle manner, but not deep enough to draw blood.

If you are worried about the scene, always communicate it to your partner. As always make sure that a safe word is used too, because if you have any qualms, you should always tell your partner before you continue.

You should finally always choose a partner you have trust and are intimate with. If you're going to do this, the last thing that you want to do is choose some random dude or woman. The problem with that, is that you get yourself. In trouble when you do that, and they may not listen to you. It does teeter on the edge of abuse.

Any Alternatives?

So if you're turned on by blood, but you're not ready to actually try the drawing of blood on the body, or any other risks, you can still indulge in the fetish. You can use a reddish liquid, such as either prop blood, red wine, or a DIY concoction, and you can use prop knives. These are good because they give you the element of knife and blood play but without the risks associated with it. From there, you should try this, and then use dirty talk. You can use dirty talk with the blood and the fake knives, and you don't even have to do bloodletting or cutting if that's what you want.

Some people like to start out with this first, but if you want to actually try this type of play, always, always be careful. It's a high-risk activity, and one that's particularly dangerous.

Now some people may think that this fetish is strange. You may wonder who has it. But remember, people are turned on by different things, and as long as they aren't directly harming anyone, there isn't a problem with it. Some like the primal messiness of period sex, and it may be something that you've wanted to try.

If you do this, do talk to your partner, and if you decide to go into heavier forms of this type of play, always make sure that you try to find a class, or a dungeon where you can try this first. The thing is, lots of times people think they know what they're doing, when they don't, and it can ultimately create a problem for you in the future. So skip out on potentially harming your sub, and instead, try to find a good class that's out there. There are BDSM classes that do help with this fetish, and ones that you can partake in, which in turn will allow you to have a better experience with this, and allow you to truly have a good experience with this type of fetish. Remember, fetishes are different for everyone, and while this may be something you're worried about, starting off slow and easing in is always something to encourage, and something that you should always do no matter what.,

Conclusion

As you've seen here, BDSM isn't something that you just see if you like, and then go through with it, lots of this does involve proper planning, understanding of what you're doing, and trust. If you've been meaning to take your BDSM play scenes to newer and higher levels, then this is ultimately the way to go.

Understanding the dom and sub dynamic is also extremely important. Remember, the sub has a lot of power, and the dom is the one to nurture that power. If you decide to go into a slave relationship with a dom, always be ready to learn new things, understand, and as a dom, take care of the sub that you have.

And, if you decide to try these heavier forms of play, always make sure you do it in a safe, and consensual manner. This is a huge part of it, and if you aren't doing it like that, it's abuse.

But, exploring your sexuality is a fun thing to do, and if you've ever been curious about exploring more of this, you should definitely consider trying new things. BDSM is really based on your imagination, what the sub is cool with, and trust, and if you've ever wanted to try new things, and you want to explore a different side of yourself, there is always that chance to, and you'll be able to learn new and amazing things from it, and different methods and techniques to give pleasure that you've never thought would be possible before.

Printed in Great Britain
by Amazon

65674485R00045